SCALING INDIVIDUALS

Management and Company Development Strategies

Andrew Benham

Copyright © 2024 by Andrew Benham

Table Of Content

-
-
-
-
-

-
-
-
-
-

-
-
-
-
-

INTRODUCTION

Scaling Individuals: Management and Company Development Strategies
What does it mean to scale as an individual? How can you grow your skills, impact, and influence in a fast-changing world? How can you manage yourself and others effectively and efficiently? How can you develop a company culture that fosters innovation, collaboration, and excellence?

These are some of the questions that this book aims to answer. Scaling Individual is a comprehensive guide for anyone who wants to achieve personal and professional success in the 21st century. Whether you are an entrepreneur, a manager, a leader, or a contributor, you will find valuable insights and practical tips on how to scale yourself and your company.

Scaling Individual covers topics such as:

- How to identify your strengths, passions, and goals and align them with your vision and mission.
- How to leverage your network, mentors, and peers to accelerate your learning and growth.
- How to adopt a growth mindset, embrace feedback, and overcome challenges and failures.
- How to communicate effectively, collaborate productively, and delegate efficiently.
- How to create a positive, diverse, and inclusive company culture that supports your values and vision.
- How to innovate, experiment and foster a culture of continuous improvement and learning.
- How to measure your progress, impact, and results, and celebrate your achievements and milestones.

Scaling Individual is not a one-size-fits-all formula but a flexible framework that you can adapt to your own context and needs. It is based on the latest research, best practices, and real-life examples from successful individuals and companies across various industries and domains. It is designed to help you scale yourself and your company to the next level and beyond.

CHAPTER 1

The Importance of Individual Scaling in Company Development

One of the biggest issues that firms confront as they develop is how to retain the quality and productivity of their staff. As the number of projects, clients, and stakeholders rises, so does the complexity and variety of the activities that each person needs to execute. This may lead to a lack of attention, motivation, and efficiency, as well as increased stress and burnout. To avoid these traps, firms need to invest in individual scaling, which is the process of allowing each person to grow and develop their skills, knowledge, and capacities in harmony with the company's objectives and vision.

Individual scaling may help both the organization and the person in various ways. For the firm, individual scaling can:
- Improve the performance and production of each employee since they are able to harness their strengths and correct their flaws.
- Enhance the innovation and creativity of the organization, as workers are encouraged to learn new things, experiment with alternative ways, and share their ideas and opinions.
- Increase the retention and loyalty of the workers since they feel appreciated, supported, and pushed by the organization.
- Reduce the expenses and hazards of acquiring and training new workers while the current ones are able to adapt and develop with the firm.

For the employee, individual scaling can:

- Boost their confidence and self-esteem as they observe their growth and successes.
- Expand their professional chances and prospects as they develop new skills and competencies that are relevant and in demand.
- Enrich their personal and professional development as they find new interests, passions, and ambitions.
- Strengthen their sense of belonging and purpose as they match their values and vision with the company's.

To execute individual scaling successfully, firms need to develop a comprehensive and strategic strategy that incorporates the following steps:

- Assess the present status and potential of each employee, utilizing numerous tools and methodologies such as performance evaluations, feedback surveys, personality tests, and skill assessments.
- Define the ideal state and objectives for each employee based on their strengths, limitations, ambitions, and preferences, as well as the company's requirements, expectations, and vision.
- Design and deliver a tailored and adaptable learning and development plan for each employee that incorporates numerous resources and activities such as courses, workshops, mentoring, coaching, projects, assignments, and challenges.
- Monitor and assess the development and effect of each employee, utilizing numerous indicators and metrics like feedback, ratings, scores, outcomes, and results.
- Recognize and reward the successes and efforts of each employee, utilizing different incentives and rewards such as recognition, gratitude, promotion, bonus, and perks.

Individual scaling is not a one-time event but a continuous and dynamic process that demands regular communication, cooperation, and support between the firm and the person. By investing in individual scaling, firms may promote a culture of learning, growth, and excellence that can help them accomplish their goals and preserve their competitive edge in the market.

Understanding Human Resources as a Scalable Asset

Human resources are the individuals who work for a company and contribute to its aims and objectives. Human resources are typically seen as an expense or a liability, but they may also be seen as a valuable asset that can be scaled up or reduced according to the demands and possibilities of the firm.

One method to perceive human resources as a scalable asset is to use the notion of human capital, which refers to the skills, knowledge, talents, and traits of the personnel that boost their productivity and performance. Human capital may be expanded by investing in education, training, development, and retention of the workforce, as well as by recruiting and employing skilled and diverse individuals. Human capital may also be used by building a culture of creativity, cooperation, and empowerment where workers are encouraged to share their ideas, learn from each other, and take ownership of their work.

Another method to conceptualize human resources as a scalable asset is to utilize the notion of human resource management, which refers to the policies, procedures, and systems that impact the behavior, attitudes, and results of the workers. Human resource management may be linked to the strategic objectives and vision of the business and can be changed to reflect the changing external and internal environment. Human resource management may also be linked with other departments and activities of the business, such as finance, marketing, operations, and technology, to create a cohesive and efficient system that supports the development and sustainability of the firm.

By recognizing human resources as a scalable asset, firms may gain a competitive edge and reach better levels of performance and profitability. Human resources may be a source of innovation, creativity, and difference, as well as a driver of efficiency, quality, and customer happiness. Human resources may also be a determinant of resilience, flexibility, and agility, as well as a driver of change, transformation, and regeneration. Therefore, firms should appreciate and nurture their human resources as a scalable asset that can help them accomplish their goals and vision.

Charting The Evolution of People Management in Modern Companies

People management is the process of managing, inspiring, and developing individuals to meet corporate goals and objectives. People management has developed greatly over the years, as the nature of work, the expectations of workers, and the difficulties of the corporate environment have changed. I will track the growth of people management in contemporary firms and highlight some of the important trends and techniques that drive it today.

One of the oldest types of people management was the scientific management method, which evolved in the late 19th and early 20th centuries. This strategy was founded on the premise that work might be examined, quantified, and standardized to promote efficiency and production. Workers were considered interchangeable pieces of a machine and their assignments, incentives, and supervision were established by management using scientific techniques. This technique was excellent for mass manufacturing and assembly line labor, but it overlooked the human and social components of work, such as creativity, autonomy, and satisfaction.

In reaction to the limits of scientific management, the human relations movement evolved in the 1920s and 1930s. This movement highlighted the relevance of the psychological and social needs of workers and the role of leadership, communication, and involvement in boosting their motivation and performance. Workers were recognized as people with distinct personalities, interests, and feelings, and their engagement and comments were appreciated by management. This method was more ideal for service and knowledge work, but it tended to disregard the technical and economic components of work, such as quality, efficiency, and profitability.

In the 1950s and 1960s, the contingency theory of management arose, which suggested that there is no one ideal method to manage people, but rather that the optimum strategy depends on the circumstances and the setting. This approach acknowledged that various kinds of work, workers, and surroundings demand different sorts of people management and that managers need to modify their style and strategy appropriately. This method was more flexible and realistic, but it also increased the complexity and unpredictability of people management, as managers had to evaluate various elements and trade-offs in their choices.

In the 1970s and 1980s, the strategic human resource management method arose, which integrated people management with the broader vision, purpose, and objectives of the firm. This strategy considered people as a strategic asset and a source of competitive advantage and attempted to develop and use their strengths, dedication, and culture to create organizational greatness. This method was more comprehensive and integrated, but it still needed a high degree of coordination and cooperation among managers, workers, and other stakeholders, as well as a clear and consistent direction and objective.

In the 1990s and 2000s, the knowledge management strategy arose, which focused on the development, sharing, and use of knowledge as the fundamental engine of organizational success and innovation. This approach acknowledged that people are the main carriers and consumers of information and that their learning and development are vital for organizational success. This strategy was more dynamic and inventive, but it also provided new issues and possibilities for people management, such as encouraging a learning culture, supporting information networks, and protecting intellectual property.

In the 2010s and 2020s, the digital transformation strategy evolved, which used the power of technology to revolutionize the way people work and communicate. This strategy permitted new forms and modes of work, such as remote, flexible, and agile labor, as well as new technologies and platforms, such as cloud, mobile, and social media. This strategy was more flexible and responsive, but it also presented new difficulties and consequences for people management, such as guaranteeing digital literacy, security, and ethics, as well as balancing human and artificial intelligence.

People management in contemporary enterprises has moved from a mechanical, one-size-fits-all strategy to a humanistic, situational, strategic, knowledge-based, and digital approach. Each strategy has its benefits and drawbacks, and none of them is outmoded or unimportant. Rather, they complement and enhance each other and offer a wide and varied repertory of people management approaches for managers and workers to pick from and implement in various circumstances and settings. People management is not a static or linear process but a dynamic and cyclical one that involves ongoing learning, adaptation, and creativity.

Navigating The Relationship Between Organizational Growth and Human Capital

Organizational development is the process of extending the capacity, breadth, and effect of an organization. Human capital is the combined knowledge, skills, and talents of the individuals who work for the company. The connection between organizational development and human capital is complicated and dynamic, since both aspects impact and rely on each other.

Firstly, organizational development needs human capital to support and lead the transformation. Human capital offers the innovation, creativity, and problem-solving abilities that allow the company to adapt to new possibilities and problems. Human capital also adds to the corporate culture, values, and vision that form the direction and purpose of development. Moreover, human capital is a source of competitive advantage since it separates the company from its competitors and produces value for its stakeholders.

Secondly, organizational expansion influences human capital in numerous ways. Organizational expansion may generate new roles, duties, and expectations for the personnel, which may require them to learn new skills, knowledge, and competences. Organizational expansion may also modify the structure, procedures, and systems of the company, which may influence communication, cooperation, and coordination among the personnel. Furthermore, organizational expansion may affect the motivation, contentment, and engagement of the workers, as they may see the growth as an opportunity or a danger, depending on how it corresponds with their objectives, values, and needs.

Therefore, managing the interaction between organizational development and human capital is a key challenge for the leaders and managers of businesses. They need to combine the demands and rewards of the expansion with the development and well-being of the personnel. They also need to promote a pleasant and supportive organizational atmosphere that supports learning, creativity, and performance. Some of the tactics that might help them do this are:

- Aligning the company vision, purpose, and objectives with the human capital strategy and conveying them clearly and consistently to the personnel.
- Involving the workers in the development and execution of the growth projects and requesting their opinions and recommendations.

- Providing the staff with enough resources, training, and coaching to help them deal with the changes and difficulties of the expansion.
- Recognizing the personnel for their efforts and accomplishments and commemorating the milestones and victories of the growth.
- Creating a culture of trust, respect, and diversity and encouraging a feeling of belonging and identity among the workforce.

By managing the relationship between organizational development and human capital efficiently, the organization may boost its performance, sustainability, and competitiveness in the long term.

Trends and Challenges in Scaling Individual Strategies

Scaling individual strategies is the process of extending the scope and influence of one's own objectives, activities, and achievements. It entails utilizing one's abilities, resources, and networks to obtain better outcomes and impact in one's sphere of interest. Scaling individual techniques may be useful for personal development, professional progress, and societal change. However, it also raises certain obstacles that need to be addressed and conquered.

One of the primary trends in expanding individual initiatives is the use of digital technology and platforms. Digital technologies allow users to access, produce, and exchange information, ideas, and opportunities with a broader and more diversified audience. They also enable people to interact, learn, and invent with others across borders and industries. For example, a person who wishes to expand their approach to increasing environmental awareness might utilize social media, blogs, podcasts, online courses, and crowdfunding platforms to reach and engage more people, as well as to work with other organizations and influencers that share their goal.

Another trend in scaling individual techniques is the introduction of agile and adaptable approaches. Agile and adaptable techniques are founded on the ideas of experimentation, feedback, and iteration. They allow people to test and modify their tactics in response to changing situations and demands. They also enable people to learn from mistakes and achievements and to adapt their plans and actions appropriately. For example, a person who wants to grow their strategy of building a new product or service might employ prototypes, customer interviews, and market research to verify and strengthen their value proposition, as well as to pivot or persist depending on the findings.

However, scaling particular techniques also implies inherent problems that need to be solved. One of the primary problems is the potential for losing concentration and direction. Scaling individual techniques may be daunting and distracting since it entails managing various activities, stakeholders, and expectations. It may also lead to dilution and dispersion of one's efforts and resources, as well as confusion and conflict among one's aims and ideals. Therefore, people need to retain a clear vision and purpose for their scaling efforts and to prioritize and match their actions and choices with their intended goals and effects.

Another obstacle is the difficulty of assessing and evaluating one's development and success. Scaling individual techniques may be hard and uncertain since it entails dealing with dynamic and unpredictable surroundings and circumstances. It may also be confusing and subjective since it relies on one's definition and perspective of success and failure. Therefore, people need to construct and apply suitable and relevant indicators and metrics to monitor and analyze their scaling outcomes and effects, as well as to identify and fix any gaps and difficulties that may occur.

Scaling individual methods is a significant and satisfying activity that may boost one's personal and professional growth and contribution. However, it also involves meticulous and strategic planning and execution, as well as ongoing learning and growth. By following the trends and conquering the hurdles of scaling individual tactics, people may achieve bigger and more significant achievements and impact in their chosen fields.

CHAPTER 2

Talent Acquisition for Scalable Growth

This is the process of locating, recruiting, and employing the finest personnel for an organization's present and future requirements. It is a strategic function that corresponds with the organization's vision, purpose, values, and objectives. Talent acquisition is vital for scalable development, as it helps the business to establish a strong and diversified workforce that can adapt to changing market circumstances, consumer expectations, and technological advancements.

There are various advantages of talent acquisition for scalable expansion, such as:

- **Improving the quality of hire** : Talent acquisition focuses on identifying the best match for the position, the team, and the business rather than merely filling a vacancy. This guarantees that the recruited person has the essential skills, competences, and potential to work successfully and contribute to the organization's success.
- **Enhancing the employer brand** : Talent acquisition helps to establish and express a good and unique image of the firm as an employer of choice. This recruits and maintains top people, as well as boosts the organization's reputation and credibility in the industry and the market.
- **Reducing the cost of hiring:** Talent acquisition uses numerous sources and ways to locate and reach out to the finest talent, including referrals, social media, job boards, career fairs, etc. This reduces dependence on other agencies and middlemen, which may be expensive and time-consuming. Talent acquisition also enhances the recruiting process by utilizing data and analytics to assess and improve the efficiency and efficacy of the recruitment efforts.
- **Increasing the retention rate** : Talent acquisition encourages a great applicant experience throughout the recruiting process, from the first contact to the onboarding and beyond. This produces a lasting impression and a solid connection with the talent, which leads to better engagement, satisfaction, and loyalty. Talent acquisition also promotes the talent's growth and career evolution inside the business, which boosts their motivation and performance.

To conduct talent acquisition for scalable development, the business has to adopt a proactive and comprehensive strategy that incorporates the following steps:

- **Define the talent needs:** The company has to identify the existing and future talent gaps and requirements, depending on the business strategy, goals, and problems. The company also has to identify the ideal applicant profile, which comprises the skills, abilities, values, and personality attributes that are relevant and desirable for the job and the organization.

- **Develop the talent pipeline** : The company has to establish and maintain a pool of qualified and interested individuals, both internally and externally, that can be tapped into when a hiring need occurs. The company may utilize numerous techniques to source and attract talent, such as employer branding, employee referrals, social media, networking, etc. The business also has to engage and nurture the talent pipeline by giving frequent and individualized contact, feedback, and updates, as well as presenting relevant and quality information, events, and opportunities.

- **Select the best talent** : The business has to create and implement a fair and effective selection process that examines the talent's appropriateness and fit for the job and the organization, as well as their potential and readiness to advance. The company may utilize numerous methods and strategies to evaluate the talent, such as resumes, interviews, evaluations, simulations, etc. The business also has to provide a pleasant and consistent candidate experience by offering clear and timely information, advice, and assistance, as well as respecting the talent's time, privacy, and preferences.

- **Hire and onboard the talent** : The company has to develop and convey a compelling and competitive offer to the talent that represents the value proposition and the expectations of the job and the organization. The organization also needs to facilitate a smooth and seamless transition for the talent by providing a comprehensive and engaging onboarding program that introduces the talent to the organization's culture, values, vision, goals, policies, procedures, etc., as well as the role's responsibilities, expectations, challenges, opportunities, etc. The business also needs to appoint a mentor or a buddy to the talent, who can give direction, feedback, and support, as well as aid the talent to integrate and network with the team and the organization.

Individual acquisition is a critical driver of scalable growth, as it helps the organization discover, attract, and employ the finest individuals that can support and accelerate the company's performance and innovation. Talent acquisition demands a planned and methodical strategy that matches with the organization's vision, purpose, values, and objectives and that offers a good and unique employer brand and applicant experience.

Identifying Talent For Scale-up Environments

Scale-up environments are dynamic and complicated, necessitating a different approach to talent discovery and development than more stable and predictable settings. In scale-ups, the emphasis is on fast expansion, innovation, and adaptability, which require a high degree of performance, agility, and resilience from the workforce. How do managers discover and develop the proper personnel for scale-up environments?

One crucial feature is to look forward and predict the future demands of the company rather than depending on its present status or previous performance. Scale-ups are always developing and changing; therefore, the skill needs may likewise alter over time. Managers need to have a clear vision of the intended objectives and the competencies and skills that will allow them to accomplish them. They also need to be aware of the possible gaps and hazards in their talent pipeline and take aggressive actions to rectify them.

Another key factor is to concentrate on the correct attitudes and behaviors rather than merely the technical abilities or certifications. Scale-ups demand talent that can handle uncertainty, ambiguity, and change and that can learn rapidly, cooperate effectively and develop imaginatively. Managers need to seek for talent that displays a growth mentality, a high degree of curiosity, a willingness to try and fail, and a love for the goal and vision of the business. They also need to analyze the cultural fit and alignment of the talent with the values and norms of the scale-up environment.

A third key feature is to be data-driven and evidence-based rather than depending on intuition or gut feelings. Scale-ups need to have a comprehensive and consistent process for talent discovery and development, employing objective and verifiable data and KPIs. Managers need to employ legitimate and trustworthy techniques and procedures to analyze the potential and performance of the talent, such as psychometric testing, behavioral interviews, simulations, and feedback. They also need to evaluate and assess the effect and results of their talent initiatives, such as training, coaching, mentoring, and feedback.

A fourth crucial feature is to employ internally and internationally rather than depending on one source of talent. Scale-ups need to use the current talent inside the firm as well as recruit fresh talent from outside. Managers need to provide chances for internal people to grow and develop, such as through job rotation, stretch assignments, and cross-functional initiatives. They also need to build a strong employer brand and value offer and utilize effective methods and platforms to reach out to external talent, such as social media, referrals, and events.

A fifth crucial feature is to be inclusive and diversified, rather than homogenous and exclusive. Scale-ups need to have a broad and inclusive talent pool that represents the variety and complexity of the markets and consumers they serve. Managers need to ensure that their talent identification and development procedures are fair and impartial and that they do not discriminate against or eliminate talent based on irrelevant variables such as gender, ethnicity, age, or background. They also need to build a culture of inclusion and belonging where talent may feel appreciated, respected, and empowered.

Identifying and nurturing talent for scale-up situations is a tough but rewarding endeavor that demands a deliberate, comprehensive, and flexible strategy. Managers need to plan ahead, concentrate on the appropriate attributes, be data-driven, recruit internally and externally, and be inclusive and diverse in order to establish a high-performing, flexible, and resilient workforce that can drive the growth and success of the scale-up firm.

Building Effective Recruiting Procedures

Recruitment is the process of recruiting, selecting, and employing the best people for an organization's requirements. Recruitment is vital for every business since it influences the quality and variety of its human capital, which in turn impacts its performance, creativity, and culture. However, recruiting is not a simple process, as it entails numerous problems and complications, such as locating the appropriate talent, decreasing prejudice, ensuring fairness, and complying with legal and ethical norms. Therefore, developing successful recruiting procedures is vital for every firm that wants to fulfill its goals and objectives.

The first step in creating efficient recruiting procedures is to determine the job criteria and the applicant profile. This entails assessing the skills, knowledge, talents, and traits that are essential and desired for the position, as well as the organizational fit and cultural fit of the probable applicants. Defining the job criteria and the candidate profile helps to cut down the pool of candidates as well as establish suitable evaluation techniques and tools.

The second stage in creating efficient recruiting procedures is to find and attract applicants. This comprises utilizing multiple channels and strategies to reach out to possible applicants, including job boards, social media, referrals, networking, events, and headhunting. Sourcing and enticing the applicants involves creativity and strategy, as well as an awareness of the target market and the employer brand. The purpose is to stimulate interest and awareness among the prospects, as well as to display the value proposition and the advantages of working for the firm.

The third phase in creating efficient recruiting procedures is to screen and choose the applicants. This comprises analyzing the applicants based on the job criteria and the candidate profile, as well as performing interviews, exams, and background checks. Screening and choosing the applicants demands impartiality and consistency, as well as a balance between speed and quality. The purpose is to discover the greatest match and the most competent individuals, as well as to exclude inappropriate and unqualified candidates.

The fifth phase in creating efficient recruiting procedures is to hire and onboard the applicants. This entails making the job offer, negotiating the terms and conditions, and finishing the paperwork and the formalities. Hiring and onboarding the applicants demands communication and coordination, as well as a cheerful and welcoming approach. The purpose is to guarantee the acceptance and commitment of the applicants, as well as to enable their integration and adaptation to the company.

Building successful recruiting procedures is an important and demanding responsibility for every firm since it influences its human capital and its performance. Building efficient recruiting procedures requires four basic steps: identifying the job needs and the applicant profile; finding and attracting the prospects; screening and choosing the candidates; and hiring and onboarding the candidates. Each level involves distinct skills and tactics, as well as alignment with corporate objectives and values. By developing successful recruiting procedures, a company can guarantee that it recruits the best personnel for its requirements and that it maintains a diverse and inclusive culture.

Onboarding Strategies for Scalable Development

Onboarding is the process of integrating new workers into a company and giving them the essential information, skills, and tools to succeed in their responsibilities. Onboarding is critical for employee retention, engagement, productivity, and performance. However, onboarding may also be tough, particularly for fast-growing firms that need to acquire and educate a large number of people in a short period of time. Therefore, scalable onboarding solutions are vital for guaranteeing a uniform and successful onboarding experience for all new recruits, regardless of the size and speed of the organization's development.

One of the main parts of a scalable onboarding strategy is to automate and simplify the administrative operations associated with onboarding, such as establishing accounts, filling out forms, and giving roles and permissions. By leveraging HR software, such as [ZipRecruiter](https://research.com/tutorials/building-a-scalable-employee-onboarding-process) or [BambooHR], firms may eliminate the manual effort and mistakes associated with onboarding and free up time for more relevant interactions and activities. Moreover, HR software may help firms manage and evaluate the progress and consequences of onboarding, including completion rates, feedback, and performance metrics.

Another critical part of a scalable onboarding strategy is to develop and deliver a thorough and engaging onboarding program that covers the core subjects and skills that new employees need to acquire. The onboarding program should be connected with the organization's vision, purpose, values, and culture, as well as the unique objectives and expectations of each function and department. The onboarding program should also be flexible and adaptive to the diverse requirements and preferences of the learners, such as their learning styles, backgrounds, and degrees of expertise. To achieve this, organizations can use e-learning platforms such as: [SchoolKeep](https://elearningindustry.com/scalable-workforce-onboarding-strategies) or [Udemy], to create and offer interactive and personalized online courses, modules, and assessments that can be accessed anytime and anywhere by the new hires.

A third crucial component of a scalable onboarding strategy is to include and engage the current workers and supervisors in the onboarding process. The onboarding process should not be perceived as a one-way flow of knowledge from the company to the new personnel but rather as a two-way interchange of feedback, insights, and assistance. The current workers and supervisors may play a significant role in greeting, guiding, and coaching the new personnel, as well as providing them with continuing feedback and appreciation. To help this, firms may employ communication and collaboration technologies, such as [Slack] or [Microsoft Teams], to develop and maintain channels, groups, and communities where the new hires can communicate and connect with their peers, supervisors, and mentors.

Onboarding is a key procedure that may affect the success and pleasure of both the new workers and the business. By implementing scalable onboarding strategies that automate and streamline administrative tasks, design and deliver a comprehensive and engaging onboarding program, and involve and engage the existing employees and managers, organizations can ensure a consistent and effective onboarding experience for all new hires, regardless of the size and pace of the organization's growth.

Leveraging Technology In Talent Acquisition

Technology may play a crucial role in boosting the efficiency, efficacy, and quality of talent acquisition. Technology may aid in numerous elements of the talent acquisition process, such as:

- **Sourcing** : Technology can aid in locating and reaching out to possible candidates via numerous channels, including social media, job boards, referrals, and talent pools. Technology may also aid in screening and filtering individuals based on their credentials, experience, and fit for the post and the business. Technology may also allow automatic and tailored engagement with applicants, such as sending invites, reminders, and feedback.

- **Assessment** : Technology may aid in assessing the talents, abilities, and personalities of applicants using numerous approaches, such as online examinations, video interviews, simulations, and gamification. Technology may also aid in minimizing prejudice and guaranteeing fairness and uniformity in the evaluation process. Technology may also provide data and analytics to measure and enhance the validity and reliability of the assessment procedures.

- **Selection** : Technology can aid in making educated and data-driven selections about the applicants based on their performance, potential, and fit for the post and the business. Technology may also aid in promoting cooperation and feedback among the stakeholders engaged in the selection process, such as hiring managers, recruiters, and peers. Technology may also aid in expediting and simplifying the offer and negotiating process, as well as the background and reference checks.

- **Onboarding** : Technology can aid in ensuring a seamless and pleasant transfer of candidates from applicants to employees. Technology can aid in providing the applicants with the required knowledge, resources, and support to prepare them for their new job and the business. Technology may also aid in engaging and integrating the applicants with the organization's culture, values, and goals, as well as their team and manager.

Technology may allow talent acquisition to be more flexible, scalable, and inventive, as well as better aligned with the organization's strategy and goals. Technology may also boost the applicant experience and the employer brand, as well as the retention and performance of personnel. Technology may be a great tool for talent acquisition if utilized carefully and correctly.

CHAPTER 3

Cultivating a Scalable Company Culture

Company culture is the collection of values, attitudes, and behaviors that determine how a company runs and interacts with its stakeholders. A strong corporate culture may promote employee engagement, customer satisfaction, and business success. However, if a business expands quickly, it may have issues in sustaining and growing its culture across numerous locations, teams, and divisions. How can a firm build a scalable corporate culture that supports its growth and success?

The first technique is to define culture in terms of clear, visible actions that reflect the company's basic values and goals. For example, if a corporation emphasizes innovation, it might identify behaviors such as trying with new ideas, learning from errors, and sharing feedback. These behaviors may be taught and reinforced via numerous channels, including orientation programs, performance assessments, recognition systems, and storytelling. By defining culture in behavioral terms, a firm may make it simpler for workers to comprehend and embrace the intended culture, regardless of their history, job, or location.

The second option is to establish an accessible, digital library of learning material that represents the company's culture and best practices. This may include films, podcasts, essays, case studies, and testimonials that highlight the company's values, aims, and successes. The learning material may also give direction and ideas on how to execute specific jobs, solve issues, and cooperate with others. By building a digital library of learning resources, a firm may allow workers to access and learn from the company's culture anytime, anywhere, and at their own speed.

The third method is to employ blended learning programs to expand cultural training throughout the firm. Blended learning programs integrate online and offline learning approaches, such as e-learning modules, webinars, workshops, coaching, and mentorship. These programs may assist workers in learning about the company's culture as well as building skills and abilities that are aligned with the culture. For example, a firm may provide a blended learning program on how to promote a culture of innovation, which can include online courses on design thinking, webinars on best practices, workshops on prototyping, and coaching sessions on feedback. By employing blended learning programs, a corporation may provide consistent and effective cultural training to a vast and varied staff.

The fourth strategy is to ensure managers persistently encourage goal behaviors via recognition. Managers have a significant role in developing and preserving the company's culture since they set the tone and expectations for their workforce. Managers may promote the desired behaviors by recognizing and rewarding workers who display them, as well as offering constructive comments and coaching to those who need improvement. Recognition may be formal or informal, public or private, monetary or non-monetary, depending on the context and the employee's preferences. By spotting target behaviors, managers may engage and inspire people to embrace and reflect the company's culture.

Cultivating a scalable business culture is a key undertaking for every company that wishes to expand and prosper in a competitive and dynamic market. By defining culture in terms of clear, observable behaviors, building an accessible, digital library of learning content, using blended learning programs to scale culture training, and ensuring managers relentlessly reinforce target behaviors through recognition, a company can create a culture that is scalable, adaptable and impactful.

Defining and Communicating Company Values

Company values are the basic concepts that influence the conduct and choices of a firm. They represent what the firm stands for, what it believes in, and how it wants to be viewed by its stakeholders. Defining and conveying corporate values is vital for developing a strong and positive culture, recruiting and keeping personnel, and attaining strategic objectives.

Defining corporate values involves a clear grasp of the organization's vision, mission, and purpose. These aspects provide direction and motivation for the organization and its personnel. The corporate values should be linked to these aspects and support them. The business values should also be relevant, meaningful, and unique for the organization and its industry. They should represent the company's identity and separate it from its rivals.

Some examples of popular business values are :

- Integrity: operating with honesty, openness, and accountability - Innovation: embracing innovation, change, and continual progress
- Excellence: producing high-quality goods and services and surpassing expectations.
- Customer focus: it is the process of comprehending and satisfying the requirements and anticipations of customers
- Teamwork: collaborating, supporting, and respecting each other.
- Diversity: valuing and celebrating the differences and contributions of all people.
- Social responsibility: caring for the environment and the community.

Communicating corporate values is as vital as establishing them. It entails making the firm's values visible, clear, and actionable for all workers and stakeholders. Communicating business values may be done via numerous channels and approaches, such as:

- Incorporating the corporate values into the firm's logo, motto, website, and social media.
- Displaying the firm's ideals throughout the company's offices, facilities, and goods.
- Sharing the business values in the organization's orientation, training, and performance management programs.
- Recognizing and rewarding the workers who exemplify the business values in their work.
- Embedding the corporate values within the organization's policies, processes, and standards.
- Aligning the organization's plans, goals, and activities with the corporate values.
- Engaging the workers and stakeholders in discussions and feedback sessions about the corporate values.

Defining and conveying business values is a key step for every organization that wishes to develop a pleasant and productive culture, attract and retain the finest personnel, and accomplish its strategic objectives. Company values are the core of the company's identity and success. They should be clearly defined, properly communicated, and regularly applied by everyone in the organization.

Employee Engagement and Cultural Alignment

Employee engagement is the degree to which people are devoted, motivated, and productive in their jobs. Employee engagement is impacted by several elements, such as the quality of leadership, the work environment, recognition and incentives and the possibilities for growth and development. Employee engagement is very strongly tied to the notion of cultural alignment, which is the extent to which workers share and support the vision, purpose, values, strategy, and objectives of the firm.

Cultural alignment is vital for employee engagement because it fosters a feeling of connection, belonging, and purpose for the workers. When workers align with the culture, they are more likely to grasp and accept the organizational goals, to cooperate and communicate successfully with their colleagues, and to serve as ambassadors and champions for the brand. Cultural congruence also develops trust, respect, and loyalty among the workers and the leaders, which are crucial for engagement.

However, attaining and sustaining cultural coherence is not simple, particularly in today's dynamic and varied corporate world. Some of the obstacles that companies encounter in developing a strong and healthy culture include:

- Defining and articulating the culture clearly and consistently to all employees, including new recruits and remote workers.
- Aligning the culture with the strategy and the market demands, and adjusting the culture to the changes and disruptions in the industry and the society.
- Measuring and monitoring the culture and the engagement levels, and delivering feedback and appreciation to the workers who display the desired behaviors and results.
- Developing and empowering the leaders and the managers who can model and reinforce the culture and the engagement among their teams.

- Addressing and resolving the cultural gaps and disputes that may come from diverse origins, viewpoints, and expectations of the personnel.

To address these issues, firms need to invest in effective employee engagement activities that can support and preserve the cultural alignment. Some of the recommended practices include:

- Creating and expressing a compelling and inspirational vision, mission, and values that represent the purpose and the identity of the business.
- Setting and cascading clear and SMART objectives that correspond with the strategy and the culture and that offer direction and focus for the personnel.
- Providing frequent and relevant feedback and recognition to the personnel and honoring their successes and contributions to the corporate success.
- Offering learning and development opportunities that may strengthen the skills and capabilities of the personnel and that can nurture their growth and potential.
- Fostering a culture of collaboration and creativity that encourages the workers to contribute their ideas, thoughts, and comments and to participate in decision-making and problem-solving.
- Building a culture of trust and respect that recognizes the diversity and the inclusion of the workers and that supports their well-being and happiness.

Employee engagement and cultural alignment are linked and mutually reinforcing ideas that may drive the performance and the success of any firm. By building and sustaining a strong and positive culture that engages and aligns the workforce, firms may achieve greater levels of productivity, quality, customer happiness, and profitability.

Inclusivity and Diversity in Scaling Environments

Inclusivity and diversity are two fundamental principles that may boost the performance and creativity of any business, particularly in growing situations. Scaling environments are ones that undergo fast development, change, and complexity, such as startups, social movements, or worldwide networks. In such contexts, inclusion and diversity may bring various advantages, such as:

- **Increasing creativity and problem-solving:** By bringing together individuals from diverse backgrounds, viewpoints, and experiences, inclusion and diversity may build a culture of learning, curiosity, and cooperation. This may help develop fresh ideas, solutions, and opportunities that would otherwise be neglected or disregarded.
- **Enhancing customer satisfaction and loyalty** : By reflecting the variety of their customers, workers, and stakeholders, inclusive and varied firms may better understand and satisfy their requirements, preferences, and expectations. This may boost customer happiness, retention, and loyalty, as well as attract new consumers and markets.
- **Improving employee engagement and retention:** By establishing a feeling of belonging, respect, and empowerment, inclusion and diversity may enhance employee morale, motivation, and commitment. This

may minimize turnover, absenteeism, and conflict, as well as boost productivity, performance, and creativity.

However, inclusion and diversity are rarely simple to acquire or sustain, particularly in growing contexts. The following are some of the potential problems that might arise:

- **Managing disputes and biases** : As individuals from diverse backgrounds, viewpoints, and experiences interact, there can be misunderstandings, arguments, or tensions that might damage the harmony and efficiency of the company. Moreover, there can be conscious or unconscious prejudices that might lead to discrimination, exclusion, or favoritism.
- **Balancing unity and diversity** : As the company expands, evolves, and diversifies, there can be a need to build a shared vision, purpose, and culture that can unify and motivate everyone. However, this could also require surrendering or sacrificing certain parts of individual or collective identity, autonomy, or expression.
- **Adapting to changing demands and expectations:** As the business encounters new possibilities, problems, and rivals, there can be a need to continually update and enhance its goods, services, and procedures. However, this can also mean modifying or discarding some of the established methods, norms, or ideals that might have been successful or treasured in the past.

Therefore, inclusion and diversity in scaling situations need careful design, execution, and assessment. Some of the tactics that can assist include:

- **Establishing clear and inclusive policies and practices:** The company should identify and convey its vision, purpose, and values regarding inclusiveness and diversity, as well as its objectives, expectations, and metrics of performance. It should also ensure that its rules and procedures are fair, transparent, and consistent, and that they encourage and reward inclusion and diversity at all levels and phases of the company.

- **Providing training and development opportunities:** The business should provide frequent and appropriate training and development opportunities for its workers, managers, and leaders to expand their knowledge, skills, and competencies related to inclusion and diversity. It should also stimulate and enable learning and interchange across diverse groups and people to build mutual understanding, respect, and appreciation.
- **Seeking and integrating feedback and input:** The company should seek and absorb feedback and input from its workers, customers, and stakeholders to monitor and assess its progress and performance regarding inclusion and diversity. It should also seek and encourage comments and proposals for development, and appreciate and celebrate its efforts and victories.

Inclusivity and diversity are vital for every firm, particularly in growing situations, since they may give major advantages in terms of innovation, customer happiness, and staff engagement. However, inclusion and diversity also bring various obstacles, including managing disputes and prejudices, balancing unity with variety, and responding to changing requirements and expectations. Therefore, inclusion and diversity in scaling contexts demand careful planning, execution and assessment, as well as the use of diverse tactics, such as developing clear and inclusive policies and procedures, offering training and development opportunities.

Sustaining Culture Through Growth and Change

Culture is the set of common values, beliefs, and behaviors of a group of people. It affects how people engage with one another and with their surroundings. Culture is dynamic and changes throughout time as individuals adjust to changing circumstances and learn from new experiences. However, culture also confronts threats from external influences, such as globalization, migration, technology, and climate change, that may jeopardize its continuity and variety. How can culture be perpetuated through expansion and change without losing its core and identity?

One potential strategy to conserve culture is to preserve and promote its tangible and intangible legacy. Tangible heritage refers to the tangible expressions of culture, such as monuments, buildings, objects, landscapes, and natural resources. Intangible legacy refers to the non-material parts of civilization, such as languages, religions, customs, arts, and knowledge. Preserving and promoting history may help sustain the historical and cultural memory of a group of people, as well as generate a feeling of pride and belonging among its members. It may also contribute to the social and economic growth of a town by attracting visitors, producing employment, and upgrading education. For example, UNESCO's World Heritage List acknowledges and preserves places of great universal worth that embody the cultural and ecological variety of mankind.

Another alternative strategy to conserve culture is to foster and support intercultural communication and exchange. Intercultural conversation is the process of communication and interaction among individuals from various cultural backgrounds with respect and mutual understanding. Exchange is the sharing and learning of cultural manifestations, such as music, literature, gastronomy, and sports. Encouraging and supporting international communication and interaction may help enhance and diversify culture by exposing individuals to fresh ideas, viewpoints, and experiences. It may also help to avoid and resolve disputes by eliminating preconceptions, biases, and discrimination. For example, the Alliance of Civilizations is an initiative of the United Nations that attempts to strengthen ties across cultures and civilizations by developing collaboration and partnerships among many stakeholders.

Culture is an important and valuable commodity for mankind that has to be perpetuated through development and change. Two potential approaches to perpetuate culture are to conserve and promote its legacy and to encourage and enable its debate and interchange. These strategies may help culture maintain its basic values and identity while also adjusting to new realities and possibilities.

CHAPTER 4

Leadership and Management
Development at Scale

Leadership and management are crucial talents for every firm, particularly in today's complicated and dynamic environment.

However, building these talents throughout the company is not a simple undertaking. It demands a strategic strategy, a scalable solution, and a demonstrable effect.

A strategic approach to leadership and management development entails connecting the learning objectives with the company goals and the organizational culture. It also requires recognizing the precise leadership behaviors and abilities that promote success and innovation in diverse situations and levels. For example, McKinsey & Company offers four principles for training leaders at scale: concentrate on the most successful behaviors, involve a critical mass of influencers, design for permanent behavioral change, and integrate the program into the larger systems.

A scalable solution for leadership and management development implies offering access to high-quality and relevant material and experiences for a large and varied audience. It also involves using technology and platforms that provide flexibility, customization, and collaboration. For example, the Center for Creative Leadership (CCL) provides many scalable options, such as online courses, microlearning modules, virtual coaching, and peer learning networks, that may reach thousands of learners throughout the world.

A quantifiable effect for leadership and management development implies measuring the results and the return on investment of the learning efforts. It also includes monitoring the progress and the input of the learners and the stakeholders and changing the program appropriately. For example, CCL employs a framework called the Kirkpatrick-Phillips Model, which analyzes the effect of learning at six levels: response, learning, application, impact, return on investment, and intangibles.

Leadership and management development at scale is a vital aspect of future-proofing of any firm. It may help to develop a culture of learning, cooperation and innovation and boost the performance and the resilience of the business. However, it takes a thorough preparation, a clever implementation, and a rigorous assessment, based on the best practices and the newest research in the area.

Developing Leaders For Scale-Up Scenarios

Scale-up scenarios are circumstances when a firm or an organization has to quickly increase its operations, client base, income, or influence. Scaling up may be tough since it entails adjusting to new markets, technology, rules, and rivals. It also needs a high degree of leadership, since the leaders need to manage the transition, encourage the team, and align the vision and plan.

One of the main parts of creating leaders for scale-up situations is to promote a growth mentality. A growth mindset is the concept that one can enhance one's talents and skills through study and effort. Leaders with a growth mentality are more likely to accept difficulties, seek criticism, learn from errors, and continue in the face of hurdles. They are also more receptive to innovation, experimentation, and teamwork, which are crucial for scaling up.

Another crucial part of creating leaders for scale-up situations is to provide them with the proper support and resources. Leaders need to have access to mentors, coaches, peers, and experts who can give guidance, advice, and criticism. They also need to have chances to gain new skills, acquire new information, and grow their network. Moreover, they need to have the autonomy and power to make choices, take risks, and execute changes.

A third key part of creating leaders for scale-up situations is to foster a culture of excellence and accountability. Leaders need to establish high standards and expectations for themselves and their team and express them clearly and consistently. They also need to monitor and assess the growth and performance of their team and give recognition and incentives for successes. Furthermore, they need to hold themselves and their team responsible for the outcomes and address any flaws or gaps swiftly and efficiently.

Developing leaders for scale-up situations is a key undertaking for any company or organization that wants to develop and flourish. It entails nurturing a growth mentality, giving assistance and tools, and building a culture of excellence and responsibility. By doing so, leaders may help their team to overcome the hurdles and capture the potential of scaling up.

Effective Management Training and Education

Management is the process of planning, organizing, directing, and regulating the resources and activities of an organization to accomplish its objectives. Management training and education are vital for growing the skills and competences of managers and leaders, as well as boosting their performance and effectiveness.

Management training and education may be offered via different techniques, including traditional courses, workshops, seminars, coaching, mentoring, online learning, and self-directed learning. The choice of the technique relies on the aims, requirements, preferences, and availability of the learners and the educators.

Some of the advantages of management training and education are:

- It enhances the knowledge and understanding of the managers and leaders about the ideas, theories, models, and instruments of management, as well as the best practices and trends in the sector.
- It increases the skills and capacities of the managers and leaders to use management concepts and practices to solve issues, make choices, communicate effectively, motivate and inspire people, assign duties, handle disputes, and deal with change.
- It encourages the attitudes and values of managers and leaders to be ethical, responsible, accountable, collaborative, inventive, and customer-oriented.
- It boosts the confidence and self-esteem of the managers and leaders to tackle the difficulties and opportunities in their positions and responsibilities.
- It enhances the performance and productivity of the managers and leaders, as well as their teams and organizations, by obtaining the required objectives and outputs.

Management training and education should be connected with the vision, purpose, objectives, and strategies of the business, as well as the expectations and input of the stakeholders. Management training and education should also be examined and assessed periodically to quantify their efficacy and impact and to identify the areas for improvement and growth.

Management training and education are constant and ongoing activities that demand the dedication and cooperation of both the learners and the teachers. Management training and education are not only useful for individual, managers and leaders, but also for the company and the society as a whole.

Nurturing Leadership at All Levels

Leadership is not a set attribute that only a few individuals possess. It is a talent that can be learned and enhanced by anybody who wishes to have a good effect on their business or community. Leadership is not restricted to the top positions or the official functions. It may be exercised at all levels, from the frontline workforce to the top executives, and from the individual contributors to the team leaders.

However, cultivating leadership at all levels needs a supportive culture and a clear goal. A supportive culture is one that supports learning, feedback, cooperation, and creativity. It is a culture that embraces diversity, inclusiveness, and empowerment. A supportive culture creates a development attitude where individuals regard obstacles as chances to learn and improve rather than threats or failures. A supportive culture also gives recognition, prizes, and resources to individuals who display leadership potential and performance.

A clear vision is one that articulates the purpose, objectives, and values of the business or team. It is a vision that inspires and encourages individuals to strive towards a common goal and a shared result. A clear vision also defines the expectations and the criteria for leadership conduct and performance. It describes what leadership is and what it looks like in the given context and scenario.

Nurturing leadership at all levels is advantageous for both the person and the business. For the individual, it promotes their personal and professional growth, their self-confidence and self-efficacy, their career possibilities and opportunities, and their pleasure and fulfillment. For the organization, it increases its performance and productivity, its innovation and creativity, its adaptation and resilience, and its reputation and impact.

Therefore, cultivating leadership at all levels is a desirable and gratifying task. It is neither a one-time event or a one-size-fits-all method. It is a constant and personalized process that demands dedication, communication, and cooperation from all stakeholders. It is a process that exploits the talents and potential of each person and harnesses the collective power and synergy of the full team or organization.

Implementing Feedback and Growth Oriented Cultures

Feedback and development are two crucial components of a strong corporate culture. Feedback is the practice of delivering constructive and timely information to workers about their performance, strengths, and areas for growth. Growth is the effect of feedback, as workers utilize it to learn, grow, and realize their potential.

Implementing feedback and development oriented cultures demands a clear goal, supportive leadership, and a continual learning environment. A clear vision helps to align the aims and expectations of the business and its workers and to express the value and purpose of feedback. A supportive leadership develops a culture of trust, respect, and transparency where criticism is regarded as a gift and an opportunity, not as a threat or a punishment. A continuous learning environment offers the resources, tools, and opportunity for workers to act on feedback, to gain new skills, and to achieve their career objectives.

Some of the advantages of establishing feedback and development oriented cultures are:

- Increased employee engagement, satisfaction, and retention. Employees who get frequent and relevant feedback are more likely to feel appreciated, engaged, and devoted to their job and the business. They are also more likely to remain and develop with the firm, minimizing attrition and recruiting expenditures.
- Improved performance and productivity. Feedback allows workers to identify and fix their shortcomings, to harness their strengths, and to improve their performance. Growth encourages individuals to develop their competencies, to take on new challenges, and to contribute more to the organization's success.
- Enhanced inventiveness and flexibility. Feedback and development establish a culture of inquiry, innovation, and experimentation where people are encouraged to test new ideas, to learn from setbacks, and embrace change. This allows the business to keep ahead of the competition, to fulfill the changing wants of the consumers, and to manage with the uncertainties of the market.

Feedback and growth oriented cultures are crucial for the success of both the firm and its personnel. By
adopting feedback and development oriented cultures, firms may create a good and productive work environment where workers can flourish and realize their full potential.

CHAPTER 5

Adaptive Strategies for Organizational Change

Organizational change is the process of transforming any component of an organization, such as its strategy, structure, culture, technology, or products. Change may be driven by internal or external reasons, such as market developments, client needs, innovation, competition, or legislation. Change may also vary in its degree, breadth, and complexity, ranging from minor tweaks to major revolutions.

One of the approach to classify organizational change is to differentiate between adaptive and transformational change. Adaptive change refers to tiny, constant, and evolutionary adjustments that help an organization adapt to its environment and enhance its performance. Transformational transformation refers to massive, discontinuous, and revolutionary changes that profoundly affect the organization's identity, basic principles, and operational model.

Adaptive change is frequently perceived as less hazardous, less disruptive, and less expensive than revolutionary change.

However, adaptive change also needs rigorous planning, implementation, and assessment to assure its efficacy and sustainability. Some of the important tactics for executing adaptive transformation effectively are:

- Aligning the change with the organization's vision, purpose, and objectives. Adaptive change should be compatible with the organization's overarching direction and purpose and serve its long-term goals. This helps to build a clear explanation and a compelling case for change, as well as to explain the advantages and expectations to the stakeholders.
- Engaging and empowering the staff. Adaptive change should entail the involvement and input of the workers who are impacted by the change, as well as the leaders who are accountable for the change. This helps to generate a feeling of ownership, dedication, and responsibility for the change, as well as to encourage trust, cooperation, and learning among the staff.
- Leveraging the current strengths and skills. Adaptive transformation should build on the organization's present resources, capabilities, and best practices and augment them with new ideas, skills, and tools. This helps to generate a feeling of continuity, confidence, and competence for the shift, as well as to maximize the use of time, money, and energy.
- Experimenting and iterating. Adaptive change should entail testing and improving the change efforts via trial and error, feedback, and assessment. This helps to develop a culture of innovation, learning, and improvement, as well as to identify and handle any difficulties, obstacles, or opportunities that occur throughout the change process.

Adaptive transformation is a critical technique for firms to manage the dynamic and unpredictable environment they operate in. By adopting adaptive change successfully, companies may strengthen their flexibility, resilience, and performance and achieve their targeted goals.

Adapting Individual Strategies to Company Growth

As a business expands, it encounters new difficulties and possibilities that demand adjustments in its strategy, operations, and culture. The same applies to the personnel that work in the organization, as they need to adjust their talents, jobs, and attitudes to the growing business environment. In this article, I will describe some of the ways that people may adjust their tactics to corporate growth and why this is vital for their personal and professional development.

One of the ways that people may adjust their plans for corporate development is by embracing learning and innovation. As the firm increases its goods, services, markets, and consumers, it has to continually innovate and enhance its offers and processes. This implies that the people who work in the organization need to be open to learning new things, developing new skills, and experimenting with new ideas. They also need to be flexible and adaptive to changing conditions and eager to take on new tasks and responsibilities. By embracing learning and innovation, people may not only contribute to the company's success but also increase their own capabilities and career opportunities.

Another way that people may adjust their tactics for corporate development is by matching their aims and values with the firm's vision and purpose. As the firm expands, it may face the danger of losing its identity, purpose, and culture, which may impair its performance and reputation. To avoid this, the organization has to convey and reinforce its vision and purpose to its workers and ensure that they share the same aims and values. This implies that the people who work in the organization need to understand and support the firm's vision and goal and match their actions and choices with these. They also need to be aware of the company's basic beliefs and principles and uphold them in their work and conduct. By connecting their aims and values with the business's vision and purpose, people may not only assist the firm in accomplishing its objectives but also generate a sense of belonging and loyalty.

The third way that people may adjust their tactics for corporate development is by cooperating and communicating effectively with others. As the organization expands, it gets more complicated and diversified, with more departments, teams, and stakeholders engaged. This implies that the people who work in the organization need to interact and communicate effectively with others, both inside and outside the company. They need to be able to operate in cross-functional and cross-cultural teams and exploit the abilities and views of other individuals. They also need to be able to communicate effectively and convincingly and listen to and react to comments and ideas. By cooperating and communicating successfully with others, people may not only increase the quality and efficiency of their job but also create trust and rapport with their colleagues and partners.

Adapting individual plans to corporate development is vital for both the firm and the people who work in it. By embracing learning and innovation, aligning their objectives and values with the company's vision and purpose, and working and communicating effectively with others, people may not only assist the company's progress but also boost their personal development and pleasure.

Managing Individual Through Organizational Change

In today's constantly competitive environment, organizational change is an unavoidable reality. However, change may also be disruptive and demanding for the people who have to adjust to new ways of working, thinking, and acting. Therefore, managing individuals through organizational change is a vital skill for leaders and change practitioners who want to assure the success and sustainability of their change programs.

One of the most extensively utilized models for managing individuals through organizational change is the Prosci ADKAR Model, which stands for Awareness, Desire, Knowledge, Ability, and Reinforcement. The ADKAR Model defines the five outcomes that a person has to attain in order to effectively accept and apply a change. By addressing the obstacles and facilitators of each outcome, change practitioners may guide and empower individuals through their transition journey from their present condition to their desired future one.

The first result, awareness, is about establishing a clear and compelling case for change, describing why the change is occurring, what the dangers of not changing are, and what the advantages of the change are for the business and the person.

The second result, desire, is about developing and maintaining the desire and commitment to participate in and support the change, taking into consideration the personal and organizational drivers and resistors of the change.

The third result, knowledge, is about giving the essential knowledge, training, and coaching to help the person understand how to change and what new abilities, behaviors, and expectations are needed by the transformation.

The fourth result, ability, is about allowing the person to exhibit and implement the new skills and behaviors in practice, overcoming any hurdles or problems that may hamper their success.

The fifth result, reinforcement, is about continuing the change and preventing the person from returning to the old behaviors, utilizing incentives, recognition, feedback, and punishments to reinforce the intended outcomes.

The ADKAR Model is a useful tool for managing individuals through organizational change, as it helps to diagnose the gaps and issues that may prevent the individual from adopting the change and to design and implement effective change management interventions that address the specific needs and concerns of the individual. By adopting the ADKAR Model, change practitioners may guarantee that the person is not only aware of and eager to change but also capable of and committed to change, thereby improving the possibility of obtaining the intended outcomes and benefits of the change.

Embracing Change and Innovation in Individual Operations

Change and innovation are inescapable forces in the contemporary world, touching every part of our lives, from technology to culture, from business to education. However, not everyone is comfortable with change and innovation, particularly when it comes to their own professional and personal routines. Some individuals may oppose change and innovation, worrying that they would lose their talents, identity, or security. Others may welcome change and innovation, viewing them as chances to learn, develop, and improve. In this article, I will argue that embracing change and innovation in individual operations is advantageous for both personal and professional growth, and I will present some techniques to assist people in dealing with change and innovation.

One of the key advantages of accepting change and innovation in individual operations is that it may boost one's creative and problem-solving abilities. Change and innovation frequently push us to think outside the box, to develop new ways of doing things, and to adapt to diverse conditions. By accepting change and innovation, we may spark our creativity, produce new ideas, and uncover new answers. For example, a teacher who supports change and innovation may utilize numerous online tools and platforms to produce interesting and interactive courses for their pupils instead of depending on conventional textbooks and lectures. A programmer who loves change and innovation may experiment with multiple languages and frameworks to build creative apps instead of adhering to the same old techniques and tools.

Another advantage of accepting change and innovation in individual operations is that it may boost one's productivity and efficiency. Change and innovation frequently provide new technology, methods, and systems that may help us execute our duties quicker, easier, and better. By embracing change and innovation, we can use these new resources, streamline our operations, and enhance our results. For example, a writer who loves change and innovation may utilize numerous tools and applications to organize their ideas, research their themes, and revise their drafts instead of depending on pen and paper or word processors. A manager who welcomes change and innovation may utilize different digital tools and platforms to connect with their team, monitor their development, and assess their performance instead of depending on meetings and reports.

However, embracing change and innovation in individual operations is not always straightforward, and it may need some changes and help. Here are some techniques to help people deal with change and innovation:

- Be open-minded and inquiring. Instead of rejecting or dismissing change and innovation, attempt to learn more about them, grasp their advantages and limitations, and explore their potential. Ask questions, perform research, and seek feedback.
- Be flexible and adaptive. Instead of sticking to your old ways of doing things, attempt to adapt your habits, rituals, and expectations to match the new reality. Experiment with multiple possibilities, explore different situations, and accept trial & error.
- Be proactive and positive. Instead of waiting for change and innovation to happen to you, attempt to start and influence them. Seek possibilities, take risks, and push yourself. Celebrate your accomplishments, learn from your mistakes, and enjoy the process.

Embracing change and innovation in individual operations may be advantageous for both personal and professional growth, as it can strengthen one's creativity and problem-solving abilities and raise one's productivity and efficiency. However, embracing change and innovation may also require some changes and assistance, and people may employ certain tactics to help them deal with change and innovation, such as being open-minded, adaptable, and proactive. By embracing change and innovation in individual operations, people may not only survive but prosper in the contemporary world.

The Role of HR in Change Management

Change management is the process of planning, executing, and assessing changes in an organization's structure, culture, or operations. Change management seeks to accomplish desired objectives, eliminate opposition, and maximize benefits for the company and its stakeholders.

Human resources (HR) plays a critical part in change management, since it is responsible for handling the human aspect of change. HR may contribute to change management in different ways, such as:

- **Change leader or owner** : HR may start and lead change programs within its own department or across the company. For example, HR might adopt new rules, procedures, or practices to increase employee performance, engagement, or well-being. HR may also integrate its strategy and procedures with the organization's vision and objectives.

- **Change advisor** : HR may give direction and assistance to other managers and employees who are engaged in or impacted by change. For example, HR may assist managers convey the reasons, advantages, and expectations of change to their staff. HR may also assist workers deal with the emotional and behavioral components of change, such as fear, worry, or resistance.

- **Change educator** : HR may plan and implement training and development programs to provide managers and staff with the knowledge and skills required for change. For example, HR may train managers on how to apply change management tools and procedures, such as stakeholder analysis, risk assessment, or action planning. HR may also train staff on how to adjust to new methods of working, such as adopting new technology, following new processes, or engaging with new partners.

- **Change participant** : HR may engage in change projects as a stakeholder, a team member, or a change agent. For example, HR may give comments, ideas, or thoughts on the change process and results. HR may also cooperate with other areas or departments to guarantee the alignment and integration of transformation activities. HR may also persuade and motivate people to accept and support change.

- **Change evaluator:** HR may assess and monitor the success and effect of change efforts using different techniques and tools, including surveys, interviews, focus groups, or metrics. For example, HR may analyze the satisfaction, engagement, or performance of managers and workers before, during, and after change. HR may also analyze the effectiveness, efficiency, or sustainability of the transformation results and outputs.

HR has an important and diverse role in change management, as it may lead, advise, teach, participate, and assess change projects. By doing so, HR may help the company accomplish its change goals, overcome its change difficulties and realize its change benefits.

CHAPTER 6

Employee Engagement and Retention at Scale

These are two fundamental aspects that determine the performance and success of every company. Engaged workers are more productive, dedicated, and loyal to their job and company, while retained employees decrease the costs and disruptions of turnover and sustain organizational expertise and culture. However, attaining high levels of employee engagement and retention may be tough, particularly for large-scale firms that operate in many locations, markets, and settings.

One of the key problems with employee engagement and retention at scale is establishing consistency and alignment throughout the business. This implies that the organization's vision, beliefs, and objectives are clearly conveyed and understood by all workers, regardless of their function, location, or history. It also implies that the organization's policies, procedures, and processes are fair, transparent, and inclusive, and that they meet the needs and goals of the diverse workforce. Furthermore, it implies that the organization's leaders and managers are qualified and empowered to promote a pleasant and supportive work environment where people feel appreciated, respected, and acknowledged for their efforts.

Another problem with employee engagement and retention at scale is offering chances and tools for staff growth and development. This implies that the business provides a range of learning and development programs and platforms that cater to the diverse abilities, interests, and career pathways of its personnel. It also implies that the business supports and enables feedback, coaching, and mentoring, both within and between teams and departments, to help workers learn from each other and improve their performance. Moreover, it implies that the firm rewards and promotes individuals based on their merit and potential and that it develops clear and realistic career advancement pathways for them.

The third issue of employee engagement and retention at scale is responding to the changing demands and expectations of the workers and the external environment. This implies that the company monitors and assesses the degree and drivers of employee engagement and retention, using different methodologies and metrics, and that it solicits and acts on the opinions and recommendations of the workers. It also implies that the business supports innovation and experimentation and that it enables workers to have a voice and a choice in how they work and what they work on. Furthermore, it implies that the organization predicts and reacts to the trends and disruptions that influence the industry and the society, and that it prepares and supports workers for the future of work.

Employee engagement and retention at scale are crucial for the long-term survival and competitiveness of any firm. However, they demand a comprehensive and holistic strategy that handles the various and complex issues that arise from functioning in a large and dynamic setting. By ensuring consistency and alignment, giving opportunities and resources, and adjusting to changing requirements and expectations, firms can boost their employee engagement and retention at scale and enjoy the advantages of having a motivated, engaged, and loyal staff.

Building and Sustaining Employee Engagement

Employee engagement is the degree to which workers feel devoted to and engaged with their employer. Engaged workers are more productive, loyal, and pleased than disengaged ones. They also add to the organization's success and reputation. Therefore, establishing and retaining employee engagement is a critical aim for every firm.

However, obtaining high levels of employee engagement is not simple, particularly in the setting of the COVID-19 outbreak, which has disturbed the work environment and raised uncertainty and stress for many workers. According to a recent poll, 55% of workers want to seek a new job in the next 12 months, signaling a possible wave of turnover and disengagement. How can firms avoid this and enhance employee engagement in these hard times?

One viable option is to follow the Employee Engagement Checklist, a research-based resource that gives practical advice for managers and leaders to enhance employee engagement. The checklist consists of three primary categories: connecting, enjoying, and rewarding.

Connecting refers to helping workers link their job with their own beliefs and ambitions, as well as developing a sense of belonging and purpose inside the firm. Some methods to achieve this are:

- Model the basic principles and purpose of the company and explain how they connect to the workers' job.

- Ask for and learn from input from workers and include them in decision-making processes.
- Provide chances for workers to interact and socialize with their colleagues and bosses, both electronically and in person.
- Recognize and honor the successes and efforts of workers and teams.

Enjoying refers to making the job itself less stressful and more pleasurable, as well as offering opportunities for people to develop and improve. Some methods to achieve this are:

- Reduce needless burden and bureaucracy and simplify the work procedures.
- Provide freedom and autonomy for workers to select when, where, and how they work, as long as they achieve the objectives and goals.
- Offer training and development programs and resources for workers to improve their skills and expertise.
- Encourage staff to take breaks and conduct self-care and wellness activities.

Rewarding refers to rewarding workers properly and sufficiently for their performance, as well as giving extra incentives and advantages. Some methods to achieve this are:

- Ensure that the compensation and benefits are competitive and equal throughout the business and reflect the performance and worth of workers.
- Provide cash incentives and prizes for personnel who surpass the objectives and goals.
- Offer non-financial benefits, such as praise, recognition, feedback, and the opportunity for promotion.
- Grant workers more time off, such as vacation days, personal days, or sabbaticals.

By following these guidelines, firms may establish and maintain employee engagement, which will benefit both the workers and the company in the long term. Employee engagement is not a one-time event but a continual process that demands regular attention and effort from all parties involved. Therefore, firms should frequently evaluate and assess employee engagement and change their tactics accordingly.

Developing Effective Performance Management Systems

Performance management is the process of planning, monitoring, evaluating, and enhancing the performance of people and teams in a company. Performance management systems are the tools and processes that assist this process, such as goal setting, feedback, coaching, evaluation, and reward. Developing effective performance management systems is critical for accomplishing corporate goals, boosting employee engagement, and developing a culture of excellence.

The following are some critical stages for establishing successful performance management systems:

- Align performance objectives with corporate strategy and vision. Performance objectives should be SMART (specific, measurable, attainable, relevant, and time-bound) and represent the priorities and expectations of the company. Performance objectives should also be connected with the values and mission of the firm and express a clear direction and purpose for people and teams.

- Involve workers and supervisors in the performance management process. Performance management should be a collaborative and continual effort, not a one-time event. Employees and management should engage in creating performance objectives, assessing progress, offering and receiving feedback, identifying strengths and areas for growth, and rewarding successes. Employees and management should also have frequent and constructive performance talks and address any problems or concerns swiftly and politely.

- Provide continuing assistance and development opportunities for workers and supervisors. Performance management should not just concentrate on reviewing previous performance but also on boosting future performance. Employees and managers should have access to appropriate and timely training, coaching, mentoring, and resources that help them grow their skills, knowledge, and capabilities. Employees and supervisors should also have the opportunity to learn from best practices, offer comments and ideas, and cooperate with colleagues and other stakeholders.

- Use diverse and balanced sources of performance data. Performance data should be gathered from many sources, such as self-evaluation, management assessment, peer assessment, customer feedback, and objective indicators. Performance data should also be balanced, meaning that it should represent both the outcomes and the behaviors of individuals and teams, as well as the quality and quantity of their work. Performance data should be accurate, valid, trustworthy, and consistent and should be utilized to influence performance choices and actions.

- Link performance outcomes to incentives and penalties. Performance results should be connected to suitable and fair incentives and penalties, such as recognition, praise, feedback, remuneration, promotion, development, or disciplinary action. Rewards and punishments should be based on performance criteria and standards and should be administered consistently and publicly. Rewards and punishments should also be timely, relevant, and motivating, and they should reinforce the intended performance and behaviors of individuals and teams.

Developing successful performance management systems is a demanding but rewarding undertaking that includes strategic planning, stakeholder participation, continual development, and alignment with company objectives and values. By following these steps, businesses may establish performance management systems that promote individual and team performance, engagement, and happiness and ultimately contribute to organizational success.

Promoting Work-Life Balance and Well-Being

Work-life balance is the condition of equilibrium between one's personal and professional lives when none prevails over the other. Well-being is the total quality of life that covers physical, mental, emotional, and social components. Promoting work-life balance and well-being is essential for both people and companies, as it may lead to beneficial outcomes such as greater productivity, contentment, health, and happiness.

One of the methods to improve work-life balance and well-being is to define clear and realistic objectives and priorities. This may allow one to manage their time and energy more successfully and avoid overcommitting or delaying. It may also enable one to match their behaviors with their beliefs and purpose and attain a feeling of satisfaction and meaning.

Another strategy to improve work-life balance and well-being is to set and maintain appropriate boundaries. This may allow one to respect their own and others' wants and preferences and prevent confrontations or resentment. It may also enable one to build and keep a supportive network of connections, both at work and at home, that can provide emotional and practical support.

The third strategy to enhance work-life balance and well-being is to practice self-care and stress management. This may allow one to manage the obstacles and responsibilities of work and life and avoid or lessen the negative impacts of stress, such as burnout, anxiety, or depression. It may also enable one to boost their physical and mental health and enjoy their leisure and hobbies.

Promoting work-life balance and well-being is advantageous for both people and companies, as it may increase their performance, contentment, health, and happiness. Some of the ways to improve work-life balance and well-being include having clear and realistic objectives and priorities, creating and maintaining healthy boundaries, and practicing self-care and stress management. By using these principles, one may create a more balanced and meaningful existence.

Retention Strategies in a High-Growth Environment

In a fast-growth environment, when the demand for talent is great and the competition is severe, keeping personnel is a significant problem for every firm. Employee retention is not only advantageous for the organization's performance, productivity, and profitability but also for the employee's happiness, engagement, and loyalty. However, keeping workers in a high-growth market takes more than simply delivering competitive wages and benefits. It also demands developing a culture that supports learning, development, recognition, and empowerment.

One of the important retention techniques in a high-growth workplace is to provide workers with constant learning and development opportunities. Employees in a high-growth workplace are generally driven by the desire to learn new skills, information, and experiences that may help them develop their careers and accomplish their objectives. Therefore, firms should give workers numerous learning and development initiatives, such as mentorship, coaching, training, seminars, online courses, certifications, etc. These programs should be connected with the organization's vision, purpose, and values, as well as the employee's interests, talents, and goals. By offering workers with learning and development opportunities, firms may boost their employees competence, confidence, and dedication.

Another retention approach in a high-growth environment is to recognize and reward workers for their efforts and successes. Employees in a high-growth setting are generally motivated by the urge to be acknowledged, valued, and respected for their efforts. Therefore, firms should create effective recognition and reward systems, such as feedback, praise, appreciation, bonuses, incentives, promotions, etc. These mechanisms should be prompt, detailed, fair, and consistent. By recognizing and rewarding workers, firms may enhance their employees morale, motivation, and retention.

The third retention approach in a high-growth environment is to empower and include people in decision-making and problem-solving. Employees in a high-growth workplace are frequently willing to take on new tasks, challenges, and risks that might help them develop and learn. Therefore, firms should promote and empower workers to engage in decision-making and problem-solving activities, such as brainstorming, ideation, innovation, cooperation, etc. These procedures should be open, inclusive, and helpful. By empowering and engaging workers, firms may boost their employees autonomy, ownership, and retention.

Retaining personnel in a high-growth environment is a key undertaking for any firm that wants to flourish and survive in a competitive market. By providing workers with learning and development opportunities, recognizing and rewarding them for their performance, and empowering and including them in the organization's operations, enterprises may establish a culture that attracts, engages, and retains people in a high-growth environment.

CHAPTER 7

Leveraging Technology For Scalable individual Strategies

Technology is a strong instrument that may boost the efficacy and efficiency of individual efforts. Individual strategies are the plans and activities that people use to attain their personal or professional objectives. Technology may allow people to scale up their tactics, meaning they can improve their influence, reach, or scope without sacrificing quality or cost. In this chapter, I will describe some of the ways that technology might allow scalable individual tactics and some of the obstacles and possibilities that result from employing technology for this purpose.

One of the ways that technology might support scaled individual initiatives is by offering access to information and expertise. Technology may allow people to learn new skills, obtain new insights, and find new possibilities via numerous online platforms, such as e-learning courses, podcasts, blogs, social media, and search engines. Technology may also assist individuals to share their knowledge and experience with others and to work with like-minded people around the world via online communities, forums, wikis, and video conferencing. By accessing and sharing information and expertise, people may improve their tactics and attain their objectives quicker and more efficiently.

Another way that technology might help scale individual initiatives is by automating and optimizing chores and procedures. Technology may allow humans to execute jobs that are repetitive, laborious, or difficult, such as data entry, accounting, scheduling, or research, by employing software, applications, or bots. Technology may also allow people to improve their duties and processes, such as prioritizing, delegating, or outsourcing, by employing tools such as calendars, reminders, project management systems, or virtual assistants. By automating and streamlining activities and processes, people may save time, money, and energy and concentrate on the fundamental parts of their plans and objectives.

The third way that technology might support scalable individual initiatives is by producing and providing value.

Technology may enable humans to generate value by developing new ideas, goods, or services that solve issues, answer requirements, or satisfy wants by employing tools such as brainstorming, prototyping, or testing. Technology may also allow people to offer value by contacting and engaging their target audience, consumers, or stakeholders by leveraging channels such as websites, blogs, social media, or email marketing. By generating and providing value, people may improve their impact, influence, or income and accomplish their objectives more effectively.

However, leveraging technology for scaled individual methods also presents certain obstacles and potential. Some of the problems include ensuring quality and consistency, preserving privacy and security, and managing complexity and change. Some of the potential includes boosting creativity and innovation, extending diversity and inclusion, and supporting learning and development. Therefore, people need to be conscious of the possible advantages and hazards of employing technology for their activities and to have a flexible and adaptable mentality to deal with the changing technological world.

Technology is a useful resource that may allow people to scale up their methods and accomplish their objectives more effectively and efficiently. Technology may offer access to information and knowledge, automate and optimize jobs and processes, and generate and deliver value. However, technology also provides certain obstacles and possibilities that require humans to be watchful and adaptive. By employing technology for scalable, personalized solutions, people may make a significant impact in their personal and professional lives.

The Role of HR and Individual Management Technologies

Human resources (HR) is the function that handles the people and culture of a business. HR is responsible for acquiring, developing, and keeping personnel, as well as ensuring compliance with labor laws and regulations. HR also plays a strategic role in connecting human capital with corporate objectives and values.

Individual management technologies (IMTs) are the tools and systems that allow individuals to do their responsibilities, communicate, cooperate, and learn in the workplace. IMTs encompass software programs, physical devices, internet platforms, and digital media. IMTs may boost the productivity, creativity, and engagement of workers, as well as promote feedback, recognition, and growth.

The functions of HR and IMTs are tightly connected since both attempt to maximize human potential and performance in the business. HR may employ IMTs to better its operations and procedures, such as:

- **Recruitment and selection** : HR may employ IMTs to recruit and evaluate applicants, such as online job boards, social media, video interviews, and gamified assessments. IMTs may also enable HR to broaden the talent pool and decrease prejudice in recruiting choices.
- **Training and development** : HR may utilize IMTs to provide and assess learning programs, such as e-learning, webinars, podcasts, and virtual reality. IMTs may also allow HR to tailor and modify the learning

material and methodologies, as well as monitor and assess the learning results and effects.

- **Performance and reward** : HR may utilize IMTs to monitor and assess employee performance, such as online surveys, dashboards, and analytics. IMTs may also allow HR to deliver timely and relevant feedback and recognition, as well as create and execute fair and transparent incentive systems.
- **Employee engagement and well-being** : HR may leverage IMTs to build a happy and supportive work environment, such as online communities, chatbots, and wellness applications. IMTs may also allow HR to elicit and act on employee input, as well as enhance employee health and safety.

However, HR and IMTs also confront various problems and hazards, such as:

- **Privacy and security** : HR and IMTs need to safeguard the protection and confidentiality of the personal and professional data of workers, as well as comply with the necessary laws and regulations. HR and IMTs also need to prevent and resolve any cyberattacks, data breaches, or identity thefts that may occur.
- **Ethics and trust** : HR and IMTs need to support the ethical principles and values of the business, as well as protect the rights and dignity of workers. HR and IMTs also need to create and maintain trust and openness with workers, as well as prevent any misuse or abuse of authority or information.
- **Change and adaptation** : HR and IMTs need to deal with the quick and continual changes in the technological and business environment, as well as foresee and react to the evolving demands and expectations of workers. HR and IMTs also need to

encourage and support the adoption and integration of new technologies and processes in the enterprise.

HR and IMTs play a critical role in increasing the human capital and performance of the firm. HR and IMTs may work together to enhance the functions and procedures of HR as well as generate a happy and productive work experience for workers. However, HR and IMTs also need to address the issues and hazards that may come from the use of technology, as well as ensuring the alignment and balance of the human and technical components in the business.

Data-Driven Decision Making in Individual Scaling

Data-Driven Decision Making (DDDM) is the practice of utilizing data and analytical models to assist and enhance decision-making in numerous fields. DDDM may help businesses achieve better results, enhance performance, and acquire competitive advantages. However, DDDM is not just significant for organizational or management choices but also for individual decisions that influence one's personal and professional progress. In this post, I will explore how DDDM may be used for individual scaling, which is the process of upgrading one's skills, knowledge, and capacities to attain greater levels of success and influence.

Individual scaling may be considered as a sort of self-improvement or personal growth, which entails establishing objectives, finding gaps, getting feedback, learning new things, and taking actions. DDDM may aid individual scaling by giving a methodical and evidence-based approach to these processes. For example, DDDM may aid people to:

- Set SMART (specific, measurable, achievable, relevant, and time-bound) objectives that are connected with their beliefs, interests, and ambitions. DDDM may allow people to utilize data to identify what they want to accomplish, how they will assess their progress, and how they will evaluate their achievements.
- Identify gaps or areas of improvement that need to be addressed to attain their objectives. DDDM may allow people to utilize data to examine their existing status, compare it with their intended state, and identify the gaps or obstacles that need to be solved.
- Seek input from multiple sources, such as peers, mentors, coaches, consumers, or internet platforms. DDDM may allow people to utilize data to ask for and collect feedback, evaluate it, and integrate it into their decision-making and action planning.
- Learn new things that are relevant and valuable for their aims. DDDM may allow people to utilize data to determine the best sources of knowledge, the most effective methods of learning, and the ideal means of implementing their learning.
- Take actions that are consistent with their objectives and feedback. DDDM may allow people to utilize data to monitor their behaviors, measure their results, and alter their plans as required.

By employing DDDM for individual scaling, people may benefit from various benefits, such as:

- Increased confidence and drive, since they can see the proof of their growth and successes.

- Enhanced creativity and innovation, since they may uncover new possibilities and solutions based on data and insights.
- Improved efficiency and production, since they can optimize their time and resources based on data and analysis.
- Reduced uncertainty and risk since they can make educated and sensible choices based on data and facts.

DDDM is a strong instrument that may allow people to scale their personal and professional success. By employing data and analytical models to assist and enhance their decision-making, people may reach better levels of success and influence in their domains.

Automation In Individual Operations

This is the use of technology to do activities that would otherwise require human interaction. Automation may be used in different fields, such as industry, agriculture, transportation, healthcare, education, and entertainment. Automation may also be utilized to boost individual operations, which are the activities that individuals conduct in their personal or professional lives.

Some instances of automation in particular operations are:

- Smart home equipment, such as thermostats, lighting, security cameras, and speakers, that can be managed remotely or via voice commands, and can adapt to the user's preferences and habits.

- Personal assistants, such as Siri, Alexa, Cortana, and Google Assistant, that can answer questions, deliver information, book appointments, create reminders, play music, and do other activities using natural language processing and artificial intelligence.
- Online banking and shopping, which enable users to manage their accounts and buy products and services without visiting physical branches or storefronts and provide features like automated payments, digital wallets, and tailored suggestions.
- E-learning platforms, such as Coursera, Udemy, Khan Academy, and edX, that allow access to a range of courses and programs and enable self-paced learning, interactive feedback, and peer collaboration.
- Fitness trackers and health applications, such as Fitbit, Apple Watch, Strava, and MyFitnessPal, that monitor the user's physical activity, heart rate, sleep quality, and calorie intake and give insights and ideas to enhance their health and wellbeing.

The advantages of automation in individual processes are many. Automation can:

- Increase efficiency and production by decreasing human mistakes, saving time and money, and improving performance.
- Enhance ease and comfort by simplifying processes, enabling flexibility and customization, and boosting the user experience.
- Expand possibilities and access by overcoming geographical and physical constraints, delivering more choices and alternatives, and decreasing prices and entry hurdles.
- Support learning and development by encouraging information acquisition and skill development, offering

feedback and direction, and fostering creativity and innovation.

However, automation in individual processes also brings various obstacles and concerns, such as:

- Loss of control and autonomy by depending too much on technology, becoming reliant or hooked, and losing the capacity to execute activities without aid.
- Privacy and security difficulties, including exposing personal data and information, being subject to hacking and cyberattacks, and confronting ethical and legal challenges.
- Social and psychological repercussions by limiting human connection and communication, generating isolation and loneliness, and hurting self-esteem and identity.
- Displacement and inequality by replacing human workers and professionals, producing unemployment and underemployment, and growing the gap between the haves and the have-nots.

Therefore, automation in individual activities should be utilized with care and balance by analyzing the possible advantages and downsides and by implementing suitable procedures and laws to safeguard the safety, security, and well-being of the users and society.

The Future of HR Tech and Its Impact on Growing Individuals

Human resources (HR) plays a critical role in every firm since it is responsible for managing the most important asset: people. HR professionals are continually seeking for ways to improve their procedures, expand their talents, and offer better results for their stakeholders. Technology is one of the primary accelerators of HR transformation, since it may give answers to the issues and possibilities that HR confronts in the 21st century.

One of the biggest developments in HR technology is the introduction of internal talent markets, which are digital platforms that link workers with internal job vacancies, projects, mentors, learning opportunities, and more. These markets strive to build a more dynamic and adaptable workforce where individuals may find meaningful employment, improve their talents, and progress their careers within the firm. Internal talent markets may also assist HR in improving the usage of current personnel, minimizing churn, and boosting employee engagement and happiness.

Another development in HR technology is the rise of artificial intelligence (AI), which is the use of robots and algorithms to accomplish activities that traditionally require human intellect. AI can complement and automate numerous HR operations, including talent acquisition, performance management, learning and development, and employee experience. AI may also provide HR with data-driven insights and suggestions, which can help HR make better choices, increase efficiency, and enhance quality. AI may also help HR to build more customized and humanized interactions with workers, such as chatbots, voice assistants, and digital coaches.

The third trend in HR technology is the optimization of existing systems, which is the process of optimizing the return on investment (ROI) from the present technology stack. HR directors should concentrate on connecting their systems, guaranteeing data integrity and security, and maximizing the full potential of their tools and capabilities. HR executives should also analyze their technological demands and gaps and hunt for innovative solutions that can meet them. HR executives should also have a continual learning and innovation approach and remain current on the newest innovations and best practices in HR technology.

These advancements in HR technology have a big influence on scaling individuals, which is the process of boosting the talents and potential of each person. HR technology may aid scaling by offering people greater opportunities to learn, develop, and contribute to the firm. HR technology may also aid growing individuals by providing them with greater autonomy, flexibility, and feedback. HR technology may also aid growing individuals by building a more supportive and inclusive culture where people feel appreciated, respected, and engaged.

HR technology is a fundamental driver of HR transformation and growing individuals. HR directors should embrace the benefits and difficulties that technology provides and exploit them to build a more effective and efficient HR department and a more dynamic and adaptable workforce.

CHAPTER 8

Measuring Success in Individual Scaling

Individual scaling is the process of boosting one's own productivity, efficiency, and influence by using numerous tools, approaches, and tactics. It is a means of doing more with less and maximizing one's potential and worth. However, how can one quantify the effectiveness of individual scaling? What are the signs and measurements that might reveal if one is growing successfully or not?

One alternative technique to assess progress in individual scaling is to utilize the SMART framework, which stands for Specific, Measurable, Achievable, Relevant, and Time-bound. This framework may help one define clear and realistic objectives, measure progress, and assess results. For example, one may use the SMART framework to establish a goal such as "I want to increase my sales revenue by 10% in the next quarter by using automation tools, outsourcing tasks, and improving my communication skills." This target is particular, quantifiable, attainable, relevant, and time-bound, and may be used to monitor the effectiveness of individual scaling.

Another alternative technique to assess success in individual scaling is to utilize the OKR framework, which stands for Objectives and Key Results. This framework may help one integrate one's vision, purpose, and values with one's activities and express one's priorities and expectations to others. For example, one may utilize the OKR framework to set an aim such as "I want to become a thought leader in my industry by scaling my personal brand." Then, one may specify important outcomes, such as "I want to publish a book, create a podcast, and speak at a conference in the next year." These essential outputs are quantitative, verifiable, and demanding and may be used to judge the effectiveness of individual scaling.

The third alternative technique to assess performance in individual scaling is to utilize the KPI framework, which stands for Key Performance Indicators. This framework may help one assess and analyze one's performance, quality, and influence on a regular basis and find areas for development and growth. For example, one may use the KPI framework to establish indicators such as "I want to increase my customer satisfaction rate, reduce my error rate, and enhance my creativity score in the next month." These indicators are meaningful, actionable, and comparative, and they may be used to monitor the effectiveness of individual scaling.

Measuring success in individual scaling is not a simple or easy endeavor since it encompasses numerous aspects, dimensions, and viewpoints. However, by employing frameworks like SMART, OKR, and KPI, one may create, monitor, and assess one's objectives, outcomes, and performance in a methodical and effective manner. By doing so, one may scale one's own productivity, efficiency, and impact to the next level and attain more success and happiness in one's job and life.

Key Performance Metrics For Individual Operations

Operations management is the process of planning, organizing, directing, and regulating the activities and resources that generate products and services for consumers. Operations managers are responsible for ensuring that the operations of a company are efficient, effective, and aligned with the strategic objectives of the business. One of the ways that operations managers may monitor and analyze the success of their operations is by utilizing key performance indicators (KPIs).

KPIs are quantifiable metrics that reflect how successfully a company is accomplishing its goals. KPIs may be employed at several levels of the company, such as the general organization, the department, the team, or the person. KPIs may also be classified into other sorts, such as financial, customer, process, or people. Depending on the type and breadth of the activities, various KPIs may be relevant and useful for monitoring the performance of particular operations.

Some examples of KPIs that may be used to measure the success of particular operations are:

- **Productivity** : This is the ratio of output to input, such as the number of units produced per hour, the number of clients serviced per day, or the number of jobs performed per week. Productivity evaluates how effectively an enterprise is utilizing its resources to create output.
- **Quality** : This is the degree to which the output of an operation satisfies the requirements and expectations of the consumers, such as the number of faults, mistakes, complaints, or returns. Quality evaluates how successfully an activity is providing value to consumers.
- **Cycle time** : This is the time it takes to complete a process or a job, such as the time from order to delivery, the time from request to answer, or the time from start to finish. Cycle time indicates how rapidly an activity is providing output to the clients or the next step.
- **Utilization** : This is the percentage of time or capacity that an operation is using its resources, such as the percentage of available hours that an employee is working, the percentage of available space that a machine is occupying, or the percentage of available inventory that a product is selling. Utilization assesses how successfully an enterprise is using its resources to satisfy demand.
- **Cost** : This is the amount of money that a business is paying or saving to generate output, such as the cost of labor, materials, equipment, or overhead. Cost indicates how economically an enterprise is utilizing its resources to create output.

By employing these and other related KPIs, operations managers may measure, evaluate, and improve the performance of particular activities. KPIs may help operations managers discover the strengths and weaknesses of their operations, compare the performance of various operations, establish objectives and benchmarks, and execute corrective and preventative measures. KPIs may also help operations managers convey the performance of their operations to the stakeholders, such as senior management, customers, suppliers, or staff. KPIs may therefore assist operations managers to maximize the efficiency, effectiveness, and alignment of their operations with the strategic objectives of the firm.

Evaluating The Impact of Individual Strategies on Company Development

Company development is the process of enhancing the performance, productivity, and profitability of a corporation. It includes several characteristics, including innovation, customer satisfaction, employee involvement, and corporate culture. However, company development does not happen by itself. It requires the contribution and collaboration of individual employees who implement various strategies to achieve the company's goals.

Individual strategies are the actions and decisions that employees take to perform their tasks, solve problems, and improve their skills. They can be influenced by factors such as motivation, personality, learning style, and feedback. Individual strategies can have a significant impact on company development, both positively and negatively.

Some examples of positive individual strategies are:

- Seeking new opportunities to learn and grow, such as taking online courses, attending workshops, or reading books.
- Sharing knowledge and ideas with colleagues, such as giving presentations, writing blogs, or participating in discussions.
- Taking initiative and responsibility, such as proposing solutions, leading projects, or volunteering for tasks.
- Seeking feedback and improvement, such as asking for suggestions, accepting criticism, or implementing changes.

These individual strategies can enhance company development by increasing the level of innovation, creativity, and quality in the products and services that the company offers. They can also improve communication, collaboration, and trust among the employees and the customers. Furthermore, they can boost the morale, motivation, and satisfaction of the employees, which can reduce turnover and absenteeism.

Some examples of negative individual strategies are:

- Resisting change and sticking to old habits, such as refusing to learn new skills, use new tools, or adopt new methods.
- Hoarding information and resources, such as withholding data, maintaining secrets, or avoiding sharing.
- Avoiding difficulties and hazards, such as selecting simple work, obeying instructions, or remaining in the comfort zone.

- Ignoring input and criticism, such as rejecting recommendations, blaming others, or defending blunders.

These individual tactics may limit corporate growth by diminishing the amount of innovation, originality, and quality in the goods and services that the firm delivers. They may also produce disputes, misunderstandings, and mistrust among the personnel and the consumers. Moreover, they may impair the morale, motivation, and happiness of the personnel, which might increase turnover and absenteeism.

Therefore, it is vital to analyze the influence of individual tactics on firm growth and to promote and reward the great ones while discouraging and rectifying the problematic ones. This may be done by employing many approaches, such as performance evaluation, feedback systems, recognition programs, coaching, and mentoring. By doing so, the organization may build a culture of learning, sharing, and excellence, which can lead to sustainable and successful corporate growth.

Continuous Improvement and Feedback Mechanisms

Continuous improvement is the practice of making modest, incremental improvements that lead to major benefits over time. It is founded on the premise that no process is flawless and there is always potential for improvement. Continuous improvement needs observation, analysis, planning, and action to find and remove waste, optimize resources, and empower workers to make changes that enhance the company's performance and bottom line.

Feedback mechanisms are vital instruments for continuous improvement since they give information on the present status of the processes, the consequences of the modifications, and the opportunities for future development. Feedback systems may take numerous forms, including surveys, interviews, focus groups, audits, metrics, reports, and reviews. Feedback methods should be structured to be timely, relevant, precise, constructive, and actionable so that they may inform decision-making and promote learning and progress.

Feedback methods may aid continuous development in numerous ways, such as:

- They may help identify the issues and chances for improvement in the current processes and assess the effect of the changes done.
- They may help align the aims and expectations of the stakeholders and convey the progress and outcomes of the improvement activities.
- They may help develop a culture of improvement where workers are encouraged to engage, share ideas, and offer feedback to one another.
- They may assist in increasing the skills and capacities of the personnel and give recognition and reward for their accomplishments.

Continuous improvement and feedback methods are connected and interdependent, since they both strive to attain operational excellence and customer happiness. By adopting continuous improvement and feedback channels, businesses may increase their quality, efficiency, innovation, and competitiveness in the market.

Creating a Culture of Accountability and Achievement

Accountability and accomplishment are two crucial characteristics of a successful corporation. Accountability involves accepting responsibility for one's actions and outcomes, whereas success means attaining the aims and objectives of the business. A culture of responsibility and accomplishment is one where everyone in the business is dedicated to providing high-quality work and achieving the expectations of their stakeholders.

How can a company establish such a culture? Here are some potential steps:

- Define the vision, purpose, values, and objectives of the company. These offer direction and purpose for the organization and its members. They also serve as the foundation for analyzing the performance and advancement of the organization.
- Communicate the expectations and standards of the company. These include the duties and responsibilities of each member, the deadlines and deliverables of each project, and the quality and quantity of the work. These should be clear, detailed, and quantifiable and associated with the vision, purpose, values, and objectives of the business.
- Provide feedback and recognition. Feedback is the process of offering and receiving constructive and timely information regarding the work and behavior of the members. Recognition is the practice of recognizing and honoring the accomplishments and services of

members. Both feedback and acknowledgment are vital for inspiring and boosting the work of the members.

- Encourage cooperation and learning. Collaboration is the practice of working together and exchanging ideas and resources to accomplish a shared objective. Learning is the process of obtaining new information and abilities and applying them to a task. Both cooperation and learning stimulate innovation and creativity and develop the talents and competences of the members.
- Hold everyone responsible. Accountability is the process of making oneself and others responsible for the activities and consequences of the job. This comprises monitoring and reporting the progress and results of the work, identifying and addressing the difficulties and obstacles, and implementing corrective and preventative steps. Accountability also entails recognizing the triumphs and learning from the shortcomings of the effort.

By following these steps, a business may build a culture of responsibility and accomplishment where everyone is engaged, empowered, and enthusiastic to work towards the shared vision and objectives of the organization.

Conclusion

Scaling Individual is a book that gives practical and insightful guidance on how to manage and improve oneself and one's organization in the fast-changing and competitive world of business. The book addresses issues such as personal development, leadership, innovation, culture, collaboration, and customer happiness. The book also gives examples and case studies from successful entrepreneurs and executives who have scaled their individual and corporate performance to new heights.

The core idea of the book is that scaling an individual is not just about growing one's abilities, knowledge, and productivity but also about aligning one's vision, values, and purpose with the company's mission, objectives, and strategy. By doing so, one may produce a good influence on the firm, the consumers, society, and the environment. Scaling an individual is also about accepting change, learning from setbacks, and enjoying triumphs. The book urges readers to embrace a development mentality, a collaborative attitude, and a customer-centric approach to achieve personal and professional greatness.

Scaling Individuals is a book that will motivate and encourage anybody who wants to push their profession and their business to the next level. It is a book that will allow readers to find their potential, realize their creativity and convert their obstacles into possibilities. Scaling individuals is a book that will explain to readers how to become the greatest version of themselves and how to make a difference in the world.